CW00557847

THE PEACE

Also by Ernst Jünger

The Storm of Steel
Copse 125

ERNST JÜNGER

THE
PEACE

*Translated from the German
by Stuart O. Hood*

INTRODUCTION BY
LOUIS CLAIR

First published in 1948

This edition © 2022
All Rights Reserved
ISBN: 978-1-954357-12-9

Cover photograph: *Nuremberg in Ruins 1945*
Public domain courtesy of Wikimedia Commons

CONTENTS

PUBLISHER'S FOREWORD
TO THE NEW EDITION

The now legendary Ernst Jünger, who died at the age of 102, had several distinct phases of his life. In the beginning of his career as a writer, he wrote of his experiences as a soldier in the First World War, and before that in the French Foreign Legion, which he ran away to join while still only a teenager, hungry for adventure. His first book, *The Storm of Steel*, remains his most popular, and has been called "the modern *Iliad*" by Dominique Venner.

In the interwar years he was a key voice for nationalism and what became known as the Conservative Revolutionary movement. In works such as *Copse 125* and *Battle as an Inner Experience*, he wrote of how his generation's experience of the war could forge in them a new, hard spirit, which would lead the way towards a national renaissance.

But like most of the other Conservative Revolutionaries, Jünger did not find in National Socialism the fulfillment of his hopes, and by 1941 it was clear to him that the entire Western world had fallen into chaos, and would need guidance if it was to survive at all.

And so, as a writer and a man of some influence, he set out to collect his thoughts on what could and should be done in order to save civilization and move forward after the catastrophe of the wars, which together form a decades long, multi-faceted conflict that Ernst Nolte has called the European Civil War.

Jünger's short book *The Peace* is a blueprint for the future of Europe, and moreover the world, for he recognizes the central role that Europe has played and will continue to play in world history. Always a deep thinker who sees into the heart of things, Jünger recognizes that what is at stake is not merely the future of his own nation but of the continent and the entire world order — which indeed was remade after the war.

The book was hardly just an exercise in speculation and theory. In June, 1944, a year after it had been completed, Jünger gave the text to Hans Speidel and other members of what would come to be known as the Stauffenberg plot to kill Hitler. It was to be given to the Allies after Hitler's death, as a proposal and basis for negotiation to end the war.

Needless to say, that never happened. The Stauffenberg plot failed, and the war raged on for another year. Most of those involved in the plot, or even suspected of involvement, were summarily executed. Jünger, however, was not. When his name came up in connection to the plot, Hitler, who had long been an admirer, gave strict orders: *"Nothing happens to Jünger."*

To read the book now is to travel back in time and perhaps to imagine an alternate world in which voices like Jünger's had carried more weight, both within Germany and outside of it. When the English translation was first published in 1948, the intention, as Louis

Clair states in his introduction, was to push back against the gross anti-German sentiment that had developed during the war and which continued to metastasize afterwards. The German nation lies at the very heart of Europe and is of cardinal importance to the European identity, as the late Jonathan Bowden always emphasized. Jünger, perhaps naively, hoped that a just peace could be achieved and that cooperation between former enemies could rebuild Europe from the ruins of the war, a Europe united by tradition and blood, and by a newfound and hard-won mutual respect between nations.

Alas, things did not go as he had hoped. The end of the war brought a victors' justice upon Germany, and the decline of the West, which Jünger and others like him had sought to halt and reverse, has continued apace.

But the thoughts and ideas that he laid out in *The Peace*, and which he continued to develop throughout his long, remarkable life, are of perennial value because they are the record of one of the West's finest minds reaching for the essence of Western civilization, what makes it distinct and great. The book also marks a turning point in Jünger's thought, as his remarks on the importance of Christianity for Western civilization anticipate his eventual conversion to Catholicism before his death. We are pleased to make it available again after many years being out of print.

ROGUE SCHOLAR PRESS

AUTHOR'S FOREWORD

The essay *Peace* was sketched out in its basic outlines in the winter of 1941, and was ready in its present form in the summer of 1943. In the meantime the situation has changed drastically, but unchanged are the curative means which alone can heal Europe and, beyond it, the world.

It is an obligation for me to thank the readers of the manuscript for the care with which they kept the secret — many of them, in spite of all the horrors of imprisonment. Especially I think of General von Stülpnagel, that knightly man, under whose protection the essay came about.

This work is to be dedicated to my son, Ernst Jünger; he also had known it. After he had proved himself — almost still a boy — in the resistance to the internal tyranny and had languished in its prisons, he fell on the 29th of

November 1944 at eighteen years for his homeland, in the Marble Mountains near Carrara. In the same way have the best of all nations not spared themselves. Their sacrifice and the sorrow they left behind will be fruitful.

E. J.

INTRODUCTION

It is high time that the moral insanity which gripped America during and after the war concerning all things German — that raving frenzy of hatred so assiduously fostered by the Emil Ludwigs, the Morgenthaus and Vansittarts — gives way to a rational attitude toward what is called, somewhat condescendingly, "the German problem."

Modern man has a fatal propensity for attempting to free himself of his own feelings of guilt, his own anxieties and terrors, by projecting them onto some scapegoat, some incarnation of absolute evil, which he burdens with all the sins, all the shortcomings that he cannot face within himself. The Jews were made to assume this burden for the Nazis; for the addicts to the Stalin myth, the "trotskyites" are the scapegoat; and for many an otherwise liberal and "normal" American, this role has of late been assigned to "the German" — a sort of corporate entity, an amalgamation of all that is hateful and despicable.

Those whose concern is with a more rational ordering of world affairs and of the body politic, whose concern is the saving of individual and collective morality from a zoological irrationalism which thinks in terms of species instead of human beings, are under the obligation to tear down the wall of hatred and distrust that now surrounds Germany and makes of it a sort of insane asylum and prison house combined. We must penetrate behind the facade which propagandists have built to discover the individual German, a person, neither "good" nor "bad," but a human being with both potentialities who will in part be shaped by the very way we act toward him. Once we have freed ourselves from a magic thinking which attributes reality to metaphors such as "race" or "national character," we begin to enter the realm of morality. Morality and rational thinking cannot be divorced. The book which I have the honor to introduce to the American public can be of immense aid in this endeavor toward understanding.

Ernst Jünger is not one of those "good people" whose goodness is somewhat boring in its monotony; in his own life, on the contrary, he has lived through, and even savored, the whole gamut of multifarious experiences that have assailed and tempted the German intellectual during the last three decades. Perhaps those who have themselves descended deeply into the abyss can report more from their descent than the simple spectator who has never but walked its edge.

Ernst Jünger never was a Nazi, yet he was in the ranks of the most extreme German nationalists; he was one of the prophets of that nihilism which has contributed not a little to the demoralization and the cynical contempt for values which characterized large parts of the young German generation of pre-Hitler days. Yet Jünger, once he realized the fruits of that nihilistic spirit which he himself was not innocent of having brought into being, revolted and turned away in disgust and shame. In 1939, shortly after the outbreak of the war, he wrote *On the Marble Cliffs*, the only great anti-Nazi novel to appear in

Germany during Hitler's reign. A few years later he wrote *The Peace*.

This short book dates from the last phase of the Nazi terror when Jünger was actively in contact with the men of the conservative opposition that made the attempt on the tyrant's life on July 20, 1944. These men, who showed to a world that had not listened to the earlier mute testimony of illegal resisters who paid for their heroism with concentration camp and gallows, that there still existed German men willing to stake their lives in the cause of freedom, found in Jünger their spokesman and their herald. *The Peace* is the most impressive document from within Nazi Germany testifying to the spirit and the reality of the "other Germany." Jünger's past does add rather than detract from this value.

It is of almost symbolic significance that one who once sang paeans in honor of the warrior, one who rejoiced in the end of individuality, who praised the advent of a new total society in which things of steel, cold mathematical formulas, would pitilessly push aside all human and humane considerations, could now write an essay which starts with a quotation from Spinoza: "The hatred, which is completely conquered by love, becomes love, and such love is stronger than it would have been had hatred not preceded it." *The Peace* represents Jünger's definite break with the values of his past, a balance sheet and a farewell, as well as a vision of things to come. I do not know any more poignant denunciation — in German or in any other language, for that matter — of the evil that was Nazism, than the first pages of this book. These denunciatory pages, full of tragic beauty and passion, will stand as the most succinct and yet most adequate description of what the barbarians from within had done to a Germany they had conquered by force and by cunning. The second part of the book, *The Fruit,* presents an outline of a positive program to save Germany, more — Europe, more — Western civilization.

The one-time herald of German nationalism now has understood that if Germany is not to become a country without history, no longer able to control her own destiny, she can be saved only through a common European effort. The European cultural tradition is by no means homogeneous, though there exist certain basic and vital common concepts. Jünger knows that the great cultural achievements of Europe are, in part, precisely based on the variety and diversity of national arts, of languages, laws, and mores; he loves the many hued shades of the European tradition — "there cannot be too many colors on the palette" — but he also recognizes that Europe will not be able to survive if she is not unified economically and technically. The hoarding of resources by each nation, the customs barriers, the trade quotas and restrictions that make of each nation an entity jealous of its prerogatives, can but lead to the collective suicide of Europe. Economic autarchy in the age of supranational planning can but lead to death from suffocation. Only if Europe becomes a united and unified economic whole can there be hope for its future, for even mere survival.

These ideas are not new. They have been stated before in more elaborate detail, yet they acquire poignancy for being expressed by Jünger in 1943, in the midst of war, at a time when Nazism still held the major part of Europe under its sway. Already then Jünger knew what most Americans slowly are learning only now, that there is no longer a "German problem" but only a European problem which, moreover, cannot be solved but by co-equal participation of Germany in the work of general reconstruction. He knew that: "The rules and usages of warfare must find no place, must not be perpetuated in the peace. If such were the case, it would be a mere illusion of peace, under which the struggle would continue — at first invisibly as civil war and foreign oppression, and then openly in new blocs of power." This insight of 1943 has not lost its significance in 1948; the intervening years of folly only add to its peculiar topical relevance.

There is much talk at this date of the reconstruction of Europe, yet one feels only too often that those who but recently have been converted to a European doctrine have been impelled by motives other than the concern for the revival and survival of European culture. *Real*-politicians who but a short while ago dreamed of the pastoralization of the heart of the continent are now concerned with reviving German industry, primarily because they wish to erect a European bulwark against the onrush of the Russian state power. Jünger, when he wrote *The Peace*, didn't think in these categories; he wrote as a European who with all the fibers of his being was tied to the rediscovered European humanist tradition, worried lest this tradition be buried in the maddening rush of competing and quarreling nationalisms, in the irrational hatreds that the war would leave in its wake. *The Peace* is the fruit of an agonized self-search, the passionate reappraisal of his own and Germany's past, by a man who after the trials and turmoils and hatreds of Germany's inter-war years has arrived at conclusions which basically contradict his earlier beliefs in the virtues of the national state and the heroic sacrifice in war. "To have peace, it is not enough not to wish for war. True peace postulates courage of a higher order than that which war demands; it is a product of spiritual travail, of spiritual strength. It is attained when we learn to extinguish the red fires within us and to free our own hearts from hate and its disruptive power."

These means which Jünger outlines for the achievement of peace are certainly not sufficient to arrive at that rational control of politics which is in tune with the demands of a new international morality. However, those who will read this little volume will find in it an incentive to overcome those hatreds, those prejudices, that add so much to create the atmosphere of impending doom under which we all labor today.

LOUIS CLAIR

New York City
March 5, 1948

PART ONE

THE SEED

"The hatred, which is completely conquered by love, becomes love; and such love is then stronger than if hatred had not preceded it."

Spinoza, *Ethics,* 44th Theorem

ERNST JÜNGER

I

Surely never before was so great a responsibility laid upon a generation of men and on its thinkers and leaders as now when the war is drawing to its end. Certainly our history has never been lacking in grave and momentous decisions. But never did the fate of such a multitude depend upon them. Each inhabitant of this planet will be affected by them for weal or for woe, and not only he but his remote descendants also.

It may safely be said that this war has been humanity's first joint effort. The peace that ends it must be the second. The builders who fashion peace out of chaos must not only test and improve the old structures, but also create new ones towering above and uniting them. On these men it depends whether good spirits will guard the new house, and whether mankind can live in it in freedom and happiness, or whether prisons and cells for martyrs are again to be hidden in its foundations as sources of corruption.

If then the peace is to bring blessings for all, it must rest upon simple and common foundations. It cannot be limited to a political or — even in the best sense of the word — to a spiritual product, but must at the same time be the creation of good and generous forces. Expressed in terms of logic, it aims at basic principles; in terms of theology, at a formula of salvation.

What then must be this way of salvation that is to guide our thoughts? This — that the war must bear fruit for each of us.

II

If then the war must bear fruit for all, we must first seek the seed from which such a harvest can grow. It cannot spring from all the forces of separation, from the persecution, the hatred and injustices of our times. That is the evil seed which has been all too freely sown, and whose last traces must be rooted out.

The true fruit can come forth only from mankind's common fund of good, from its soundest core, from its noblest, most unselfish stock. It is to be sought where, without thought for himself and his own weal, man lives and dies for others and sacrifices himself for them. And that has happened abundantly; a great treasure of sacrifice has been gathered as a basis for the re-building of the world.

The sacrifice — and this everyone must have felt — lay in the unreserved effort of the most lowly and simple. Affairs had taken a driving and evil course to which there contributed the missed opportunities and errors not of the living only but of many generations. They drove on towards the fire; in fire they wished to be refined and purified. Then even those most firmly resolved yet to direct things to a good end found themselves pushed to the edge. Now for the unnumbered and unnamed one thing alone remained — to shoulder their burden honorably at the post where fate had placed them.

And in the memory of furthest ages this great spectacle will remain: how in every land, when the hour had come, they went out to battle on the frontiers, to sea-fights on the oceans, to deadly encounters of squadrons in the air. Then in every people and in every army there were deeds of wonder and to spare, and long-established fame in . arms acquired its meed of new laurels. In this battle of giants each opponent could be proud of the other; and to the extent that time tempers enmity the secret respect and even the secret love between conqueror and conquered will grow. The one gains meaning from the other.

Behind the bloody battle lines, which for the first time welded the earth's ball with glowing bands, stretched the grey lightless depths of the army of workers. In them the greatest sum of human endeavor was produced that men have ever harnessed to one end. In fulness of gratitude and of emotion one must remember these men and women, their laborious days in gloomy workshops, their night watches in the darkened towns and their long hours of work with hearts filled with care for brothers, sons and children. There is no reckoning those who died thus, worn out with overwork, bowed down with burdens and care, snuffed out like nameless lights.

The good seed that was there ground down must not be lost; it must for long furnish us with bread. That will come about only if we grasp the true and hidden significance of their labor and sacrifice. It is not that they fashioned the instruments of death and destruction, the weapons for killing, for sinking ships, for destroying city after city. Deep in their hearts there lived instead a sense of true generosity, true sacrifice, which flowers and bears fruit more richly than in the world of hate.

Under a just peace, then, we must unite what has flowed from separate but pure sources. Through reason we must give reality to something that existed as a vague force in the aspirations of unnumbered millions, whatever the land in which they chanced to be born — a greater and better rule of peace.

III

When we review the sacrifice we must not forget those who were plunged into the depths of pure sorrow, of pure suffering. The times lay upon the weak and innocent with the weight of iron.

Who knows the hosts of those who died from hunger, disease, exhaustion, from lack of care and medicaments? And those other hosts destroyed when the towns were laid in ruins, who fell beneath the wreckage of their houses, who drowned in the cellars, who suffocated or were consumed by liquid phosphorus? The line of women, children and aged who vanished thus is endless. Untold numbers had their days cut short; as many again were never to know what life is. The young grew up in hells, in realms fit rather for the habitation of demons than of men, and the children gained their first images from a world of terror. They heard the howling of the sirens before the peal of the bells, and their cradle was nearer the fire than the light.

We must think too of those who went down with the ships, who drowned in the solitude of the seas, who froze in the icy waters or whom death overcame in scalding steam, in the flare of the explosion, in the rings of burning oil spreading wide round their boats. In those days darkness lay over the paths of the sea.

Yet even the soldier had to bear burdens far exceeding those of his calling and those befitting opponents within the Christian community. This can be grasped only by those who conceive of the struggle not as a trial of arms between peoples and states, between nations and races, but rather as a universal civil war which split the world into mysterious, all the more terrible fronts.

This explains why in the course of these fateful years engagements were to take place which were far more terrible than the battles of matériel and fire of the first world war. For the man who believes he fights for ideas and ideals is possessed by greater ruthlessness than he who merely defends his country's frontiers.

So battles were made possible in which even the defeated, the unarmed could not count on mercy — encirclement and captivity which offered no prospect of escape. Over wide plains and fields the terrors of the elements vied with a technology of murder and unshakable cruelty. There were areas where men destroyed each other like vermin and broad woods in which to hunt men like wolves. And one saw, cut off from all hope as if on a dead star, great armies go to their death in the horror chambers of the pocket battles.

Numberless were those who experienced the bitterness of dying in beleaguered outposts where one sees death approaching inexorably from afar. Happy could be he who recognized the real enemy in his opponent and could fall before doubt awoke in his breast. Yet many, and they the best, bravest and wisest, saw themselves marked down for destruction, unable to yield themselves to the magic of the flags and symbols under whose influence they were doomed to give their lives. For it was these who could not escape the thought that they were in a battle for higher things than the frontiers of the fatherland — that in this fratricidal war a new purpose was being born to the earth and that many of those on the other side, whose approach meant death, were closer to the higher goal than the comrades at one's side: yet with them one had to keep faith.

So, above all for the true and pure of heart, the war entered the realms of tragedy and to an upright mind the contradiction between the voices of future and past, between the world and one's native land, between duty and intuition seemed insoluble. There were many to whom death in the open field, in honorable combat, seemed the only, the best solution. With them the best, full seed fell into the ground.

IV

Even more somber becomes the picture of suffering in those places where the world was turned into a mere slaughterhouse, to a flayinghouse whose stench poisoned the air far and wide.

In the forcing-house of war and civil war the great theories of the past century bore fruit as they were applied in practice. Now it became clear that irrespective of whether they heralded the equality or inequality of man, they had invented cold-blooded reasoning.

The yardstick of theory was applied to individuals, to races, to peoples. As always in such cases the thirst for blood soon passed all measure once the first victim had fallen.

So in the senseless interplay of force and terror, persecution and injustice broke over wide and ever growing expanses of the globe. Soon the last free voices had to keep silence, and even the sounds of terror died away in the terrible stillness which surrounded prison and cemetery. Only dark rumors hinted at the gruesome revels where police and torturers feasted on the humiliation, on the blood of their victims. For distant ages these will remain our century's blot of shame; no one will be respected whose heart and eyes were insensible to what happened there. This is above all true for the military youth, for the protection of the weak and helpless will always remain the highest flower of knighthood. No one can be a hero before the enemy whom this flower does not adorn.

From the Far East to the Hesperides, from the South to the White Sea, we learned what burdens and sorrows men bore in lands where terror was the highest law. Wars brought it in their dark train no less than civil wars, and under the domination of classes, parties or foreign armies only the aims altered, never the unchanging face of tyranny. And as in great conflagrations now one wind and now another feeds the flames, there were lands where white and red terror alternated and where the victims fell now under the blows of native despots, now under those of a foreign power. So violence raged like a plague whose germs continually inflame new hate and, spreading by many routes, strike always at the poor and weak. And however the ideas may be disguised in whose name heads are called for — the great mass graves are all the same.

Such too was the fate of innumerable nameless men who clung to lost outposts until their hour of terror struck. The doomed member of the resistance faced the omnipotence of the executioner, and the way to the peaks of suffering had many stations. Particularly terrifying were the cold mechanics of persecution, the considered technique of decimation, the tracking and surveillance of the victims by means of the lists and files of a police force which swelled into armies. It seemed as if every method, every discovery of the human mind had been transformed into an instrument of oppression.

Thus years and decades of terror broke upon countless families. House and cottage lay defenseless at the mercy of class and racial hatred, of unconcealed despotism and even of naked bestiality. And this spreading gloom was not confined to the limits of the continent but penetrated into lands which for centuries had been distinguished by legal knowledge and the exercise of justice — lands where from ancient times freedom had found as good a dwelling-place as it may have among men.

But now the mist came down, bringing with it the silence of the oppressed, over whose helplessness the tyrants triumphed with wild unbridled glee. Things lost their cheerful hue and with each new morning came the question: Would evening find the family united round the table or torn apart, its members dragged away? And when at night the light was extinguished, the ear strained to catch the whispering of the police agents without, waited for the door to resound with blows as a sign that the hunters had tracked down their prey.

These were years when even the prisons no longer sufficed, and in which multitudes, dragged off illegally and without sentence, languished in dungeons where death was the only kindness. Many were seized on the steps of the court which had just acquitted them. The camps filled, too, where forced labor ceased only with annihilation — thus achieving its deliberate aim. Anyone who there wasted away had long been dead to his kin, for the precautions designed by warped minds saw to it that no sign of life came from the torture cells.

And more obscure, more gruesome than ever before was the death the executioners prepared for the innocent after they had broken up the families and robbed them of possessions and liberty. The secrecy, the shunning of the light, the slaughterings in cellars and evil places and the hasty, unceremonious burial of the victims showed only too dearly that here was no execution of just sentence, but mere outrage and wanton murder.

The number of Golgothas where the disenfranchised were slaughtered is enormous. The crime of which the unfortunates were accused was merely that of existing, the stigma of their birth. They fell because they were sons of their people, of their fathers, of their race, as hostages, as adherents of a disinherited creed, as disseminators of their faith, which laws invented overnight had decreed to be a mortal taint.

From out of this waste of suffering there rise somberly the names of the great seats of murder where in a last and final frenzy they attempted to root out whole peoples, whole races, whole classes, and where leaden tyranny in league with technical efficiency celebrated endless bloody nuptials. These dens of murder will haunt man's memory to the end of time; they are the true monuments of this war as once before were Douaumont or Langemark. But those were names which could mingle pride with suffering; here only sorrow and humiliation remain, for the desecration was such that it touched the whole human race and no man can free himself from complicity. That was where progress led with its theories and ideas; into these swamps emptied an all-too-clever, inventive age.

If ever new pride fills us at the length and boldness of our flight, at our intellectual wings, our pinions of steel, it should suffice to cure us for a glance to be cast on the hordes driven like cattle to the graveyards and cremation ovens where the executioners waited. There they were stripped of their rags and slaughtered like shorn sheep. They were forced even to dig their own graves, if their murderers did not fill quarries and pit-shafts with the corpses which piled up too fast These scenes of horror, of which dark rumors passed from mouth to mouth, will be brought to light only when the lost souls who played the hangman there, together with their superiors, are forced to break silence before the courts.

Yet when we look upon these places of martyrdom let us do so frankly and with clear judgment. It was the evil spirit of the rabble which there in darkness practiced its grisly arts. Then we saw the feigned indignation of other evil forces which came to the haunts of infamy to exhume the hastily buried victims and expose the wasted corpses, to measure, count and reproduce them as served their ends. They played the accusers only to acquire the right to still baser vengeance which they sated in similar orgies.

Thus one massacre was succeeded by another baser still. But the hand that would help mankind and lead it out of its follies must be unstained by crime or deeds of violence.

V

The realm of suffering has a strict hierarchy with ranks, branches and gradations by which man descends. It is here that he seeks the sources of life, and as springs flow into lakes and thence into seas, so sorrows gather in ever larger volume and in greater purity. Just as for thoughts there is consciousness, so for sufferings there are modes in which they become rational and unite to acquire a deeper meaning.

Therefore through these years the suffering of the man of the spirit has been great. Far more than by his own persecution he was sickened by the spectacle of baseness gaining the mastery. It was not wars or dangers that caused him to fear, but the blind urge which drove the masses — at first in wild exultation and then in a passion of hatred and revenge — along unknown paths which soon led to the flames.

He also saw, sooner and more clearly, how man's high sense of duty was perverted, how labor and science turned to the service of death, how the sword shielded injustice, how the judge — under the crude disguise of ceremony — debased justice into a tool of the courts, how the teacher destroyed the divine image in the children instead of illumining it, and how doctors, instead of healing, maimed the weak and killed the sick.

He saw the machine arise to domination in cold structures which a titanic will forced up over night as palaces of destruction and

Babylonian confusion. All too soon they were to be seen rising like spectral skeletons from the scorched earth to herald the triumph of death. In the same way one builds into a bridge the demolition chambers for blowing it up.

He was therefore less affected by the collapse of scaffoldings and facades than by the loss of old heritage, of well-formed things handed down and irreplaceable. With each conflagration he saw the world grow poorer, and jewel after jewel fall from its crown and adornment of intellectual splendor.

He saw the old guilt mingle with new, justice and injustice so entwined that there had to come a purification by fire. Like a lofty mirror reflecting images and figures, his spirit endured and shared in silence the flames and sufferings of the blazing world.

Once more, and that in the lowest pit of all, these sorrows were finally reproduced in the mothers; in all lands their suffering was one and the same. Like Niobe they saw their children die from the keen arrows fate shot out of the unknown. Multitudes had thus to

give their most beloved, and with each mouth
the great struggle lasted a lamentation swelled
that will not die away for years and scores of
years to come.

VI

The second round of this great struggle,
which has its roots in the rise of a new order, a
new unity, was harder, more demanding, more
merciless than the first. Yet that had seemed
unsurpassable in violence and scope. The
cause is not to be sought in a divergence of
the peoples' aims during the brief truce. On
the contrary, their goals grew closer, fusing at
the focal point where a new character takes
shape — the character of work, which sets its
stamp upon the peoples and conceals their
differences. Therefore it is no longer national
aims which are in question, but the aim of the
war itself. For this reason the suffering pierced
deeper, harrowed the hearts more; for to the
horrors of war were added those of fratricidal
strife, of civil war, which are more horrible
still. In their train come yet greater perils, and

here one saw many draw back who had proved their valor on the field of battle.

Therefore the figure symbolizing the second war of nations will have deeper origins than that of the first. Then it was the unknown soldier to whom monuments were raised in the heart of every capital as a sign that the great treasure of suffering he had gathered in the fire should henceforth be the center of the nation, warming and shedding light, just as the hearth is the center of the home. And in fact an image did arise for the nations with power to form and unite in an age poor in true vitality.

But this time the suffering was more widely spread, more obscure and complex; it reached deeper into the realms of motherhood. It was closer to the great religious images. For that reason it will form the base for structures towering higher into the light. Just as the sacrifice embodied in the unknown soldier inspired the peoples, so the new sacrifice will shed its influence and creative power far over the frontiers between the nations.

Later when the fighting has died down, people will understand that reason could recognize the new ways of life and strive towards them, but that for their creation there was. required the combined effort of passions, suffering and the fire. The complexities of the fronts concealed from those who were active and those who suffered the unity of the great work under whose spell they played their parts — yet through their creative power, through the transformation into sacrifice it will become evident. Thus by falling they became the good seed which will bear fruit a hundredfold.

PART TWO

THE FRUIT

"Not in the even course of the bourgeois world, but in the thunder of the Apocalypse are religions reborn."

Walter Schubart, *Europa und die Seele des Ostens*

I

We have seen the victims of this war. To their somber ranks all nations added their contingent. All shared the suffering and therefore the peace must bear fruit for them all. That is, this war must be won by all.

That is not to say that there will not be conquerors and conquered. On the contrary, it is desirable that there should be a clear decision by arms and that no corner should remain unpurged by fire. Once matters have been referred to the jurisdiction of force as the court of lowest appeal, they must remain there pending an unequivocal decision. The more clearly, the more mathematically the logic of force finds expression, the more deeply it convinces those who recognize no other arguments, the more surely will the foundations of the peace be secured. Weapons must create an opportunity for a decision to be made, for the mind to plan. In that sense it is better for man to suffer longer than to postpone part of the process and return to the old world. As all those taking part must have grasped, there is no compromise in the race towards the goal.

The peace cannot be a peace of compromise.

II

But just as little may the peace be one of violence. The rules and usages of warfare must find no place, must not be perpetuated in it. If such were the case, it would be a mere illusion of peace, under which the struggle would continue — at first invisibly as civil war and foreign oppression, and then (as the world disintegrated) openly in new blocs of power. Therefore it is important both for the vanquished and for the victors that solid and enduring agreements should be reached, dictated by reason and not by passion.

Admittedly that seems difficult after years of total war which created enmities of a bitterness unknown before to peoples with old civilizations. And yet these years in many ways made the opponents more alike. The transformation of the world, first evident as a leveling process, made further progress. As in the first world war the monarchies were conquered by the democracies, so in this second and greater struggle the old-fashioned national states will be vanquished by the imperial powers. As a step towards this, the national element in the peoples is being consumed by fire — one of the ultimate sacrifices and one which cannot be repeated in this form. The positive aspect of this process is that it loosens the old frontiers and makes possible spiritual planning which oversteps their confines.

The course of the great evolutionary process, the dominant spirit of the age, aims at consolidation. We may hope that the peace which ends this conflict will be more enduring and bring greater blessings than that which terminated the first world war. For then development was towards the formation of national democracies and thereby towards the demolition of whatever old binding structures still remained in Europe. The new formation of empires, on the other hand, tends towards synthesis, towards coalition. That is a token that in general we are entering a period of better weather with a rising glass.

III

But how is it possible for the war to be won by all — that is, for it to be lost by none? First the question arises, what is the mark of a victorious war? The answer is this: victory is thus distinguished, that through it one's native land becomes greater and mightier.

If from the ashes of this war all countries must arise greater and mightier it is obvious that this is not possible on the plane on which the war broke out. Gains in territory and power by some must not be acquired at the expense of others.

The nations must not, therefore, acquire new territories at the cost of others: their aggrandizement must rather take place with the assent and aid of all concerned. That is, the old frontiers must be broken down by new alliances, and new, greater empires must unite the nations. This is the only way in which the

fratricidal struggle can be concluded justly
and to the advantage of all.

Today, if ever, the hour for union has come
and with it the hour when Europe, founding
itself on the union of its peoples, attains
sovereignty and constitutional form. The
desire for unity is older than the crown of
Charlemagne, but it was never so burning, so
urgent as in our time. It lived in the dreams of
the Caesars and in the great theories with
which man's spirit strove to mould the future,
and yet neither will-power nor intellect alone
is destined to give it reality. Only experience
can force mankind to take the necessary step.

Certainly the picture presented by the
world teaches even the dullest eyes that new,
stronger unity is more necessary, more
important than bread. It also seems
unthinkable to return to the conditions from
which we have come; the peace must be
unshakably secured. That is possible only by
means of treaties of the highest order, which
in their nature resemble the marriage
contract; unions of body and possessions

whereby the nations themselves are dowries for the new dwelling that now becomes theirs.

Two roads are opening up before the nations. One is the road of hate and retribution, and it is certain that on it, after a brief period of exhaustion, the struggle will flare up anew and more fiercely than before, to end in universal destruction. The true road, on the contrary, leads to unity; the forces which consumed each other in deadly opposition must unite for the new shape of things, the new life. Here alone are the sources of true peace, of prosperity, security and strength.

IV

That this war must be won by all signifies, then, that none must lose it. Even today it is possible to foretell that if it is not won by all, it will be lost by all. The destinies of the nations have been closely entwined, have become inseparable, and peace will lead them either to a higher order or to increasing destruction.

Therefore whoever emerges from the struggle as victor bears a heavy responsibility.

The logic of pure violence must come to an end so that the higher logic of alliance may be revealed. The world war will reach its conclusion only when it is crowned with universal peace and thus gives meaning to the sacrifice. That demands an ascent to other, higher principles, the ascent from the fire to the light.

Here the transition offers the greatest difficulty — particularly the period which falls between the capitulation and the completion of the peace. Then there will always be forces which strive to perpetuate the spirit of dissension. The less effective such an attempt is, the more enduring will be the peace.

If this war must be won by all, and that alone leads to salvation, then victory in battle must entail responsibility: by victory gains are won which must be shared among all the nations. Therefore to fulfil the great plans of peace, goodwill must take its place beside the spirit which in time of war was inspired by passion. War is won in opposition; the peace will be won in collaboration.

That is particularly true of this war; the stakes were so great that no compensation can be adequate. The enemy must be entirely at the mercy of the victor — but that can come about only with his assent, with his compliance.

In this sense the greatest conquest is to be found in alliance.

V

The pattern of the war itself foreshadows unification. It is the second world war, and more strikingly than in the first it appears that this is no conflict to which a boundary can be set, but that all nations of the earth are involved in it and suffer from it. That is no mere chance; it is a sign that the world is striving towards a new pattern and a new character as man's common fatherland. For the first time, the earth as a globe, as a planet, has become a battlefield, and human history presses on towards a planetary order. That is being prepared by the division of the earth into great territories.

As sons of the earth we are involved in the civil war, in the fratricidal strife. The lands we know are a battlefield as in the great disorders from which the Roman Empire arose. In this sense it is no mere chance that we live in the heart of the conflagration; we are in the midst of the fusion, the pangs of birth.

Nor is it fortuitous that it is in our lifetime that the great struggle spans the globe. For long our ideas and actions, our most secret thoughts and desires have tended towards unity. It finds expression in technical achievement, which is knowledge and desire made concrete. Its instruments are conceived by an intellect of wide vision, are adapted to great expanses of territory and are moreover too massive to serve the old-fashioned nations. The earth's ball, which can be flown over in a few hours and spanned in seconds by pictures, signals and orders, lies like an apple in the hand of man.

There is no more outstanding sign of the spirit whose aim is unity than that man, in spite of his frontiers and barriers, is acquiring a new character. One might say that he is being shaped by wonderful processes into a citizen of new empires. It is a phenomenon whose causes lie deep. It is the great transformation of our age, its inner process, which dictates all external forms. It will fuse elements from the most varied sources even if the will resists.

VI

The reasons why the formation of great empires must come are spiritual by nature and are based on the principles of the age. They are apparent in the details of our life, and first and foremost in negative, unwholesome aspects, in want. The old garb has grown tight for the movements of the new body.

As far as the symptoms are concerned, they have long been familiar. They are particularly evident in the fact that technical equipment of the various states, as inherited by us, has become inadequate. The increase in population and in energy presses the old framework to the bursting point. As means of production grow, industries clash; armies of workless alternate with armies of armament workers. Thus we see men and machines fully employed only when the aim is destruction. Trade cannot distribute evenly the goods industry produces; at one place machines stand still and hands lie idle for lack of work, while in other parts of the world the barns are bursting under the weight of the harvest and the surplus is thrown into the sea or fed to the fire.

Nor are communications less ready for wider development. In their methods and routes, spatial thinking and determination to reach beyond all frontiers find their chief expression. What the steam-engine, coal, railways, and telegraphy were for the development and unification of the national state, electrical science, the combustion engine, flight, radio, and the forces streaming out of the atom are, in their turn and at new levels, in other spheres. It follows that complaints are being renewed that the old world has become too small. Frontiers, variations in political and economic forms which hinder the exchange of men and goods, deny free passage to the many means of communication.

That is particularly true of Europe, which is rich in old heritage, and in its manifold divisions bears the mark of history's sufferings and experience. Thus it becomes understandable that from its center the great wars have flared out to lay waste the world; it is at the weakest part of the body, which is, however, also its heart and vital point, that its sufferings become apparent. For that reason this is also where healing must begin.

Europe must become a partner in the great empires which are forming on this planet, and are striving towards their final form. It must share in the higher freedom won in the face of an inheritance of restricted space.

Admittedly Europe's declaration of independence entails a spiritual act. The continent must simultaneously free itself of much that has become fossilized, particularly in modes of thought and old hatred — for that very reason the victory will bear fruit for all.

The earth will share in it.

VII

The human spirit has long felt that change was necessary. But such is man's nature that for him to take the necessary action more than insight is required — above all, it is experience that teaches.

Therefore theoretical strivings to produce — even spatially and in terms of territory — the unity which the spirit recognized and demanded, were inadequate. That is reflected in the development of the principles of 1798, which won spiritual victory but were a military failure. The armies which then marched out carried with them a more than national duty, which was thoroughly understood and shed favor on their route.

For this reason secret shrines in honor of Napoleon have been maintained in all lands — for in that prince the old dream of one great monarchy had seemed to be realized. Yet in the course of his wars, of his meteoric career, there was more sowing of new seed than reaping of its crops — and young states blossomed out of the shattered earth. After him, rigidity set in and the Congress of Vienna confirmed the frontiers in terms of the old legitimacy.

The second great opportunity to weld Europe was offered by the Peace of Versailles. But unfortunately instead of leading to new ordered ways of life it increased the sources of conflict. It remained — considered structurally — an imperfect work and can hardly be said to have brought the war to a conclusion. The First and Second World Wars are connected like two fiery continents, linked rather than separated by a chain of volcanoes. That part of the peace treaty which was devoted to general matters remained partly rhetorical facade, partly empty theory.

The concept of the League of Nations, although obscurely formulated, could have been fruitful for all peoples if its dominant idea had been applied to-individual questions. Admittedly that would have postulated the creation of a supreme body with wide powers both in legislation and government. Instead there arose a phantom body suited primarily for legal arbitration, a mere shadow, a powerless forum for disputes which throve apace — for while the structure of the peace lacked fertile cells it contained an astonishing number of details which ingeniously defined the new frontiers, the burdens laid upon the conquered and the guarantees exacted. Thus this peace shared the lot of all products in which heart has too little scope and reason too much; it shed no blessing and even the victor after a brief period of rejoicing had little pleasure in it.

It had, too, an unhealthy poisoning influence on the internal politics of those States which it treated as of secondary rank; it fed the lowest emotions — revenge and blood hatred — and brought grist to the mills of demagogy. Looking back we see how slight was any benefit conferred by this peace compared to the harm it caused to all. Thus the source from which the second world war flared up was Danzig and its ownership — towns of this rank were later to be burned down in a single night.

The Peace of Versailles had merely made the frontiers more obvious. The dislocation of economy, currency and trade, no less than rearmament, which, after a brief respite, was more threatening than before, all point to the collapse of the continental policy, which was splitting more and more into its component states. Then unmistakably the signs of the second war appeared bringing fear to men, but forcing them on, too, under a fatal spell toward that war.

Even at this stage an event could have occurred which would have been comparable to the convocation of the Estates in 1798; and for the American President it will always remain a title to honor that he gave utterance to this idea. Admittedly such a conference might have postponed the ordeal by fire, but not averted it. Alterations of the kind required here needed more than a reformation — they demanded revolution. They pushed the parties on to final clarification, to the purification by fire. As always in such cases, the dark compelling forces and not the voices of reason were decisive.

VIII

When weapons eventually took up the argument, there was still in 1940 an opportunity to avert the worst consequences. Great portions of the earth were as yet undisturbed; others had been set free from the chains of Versailles and the road thus cleared for further development. Moreover — if not *de jure* then certainly *de facto* — the frontiers had fallen throughout a great part of Europe and the people thirsted for security. At this point a just solution could have been found whereby the illusion of unity which force had produced would be replaced by unity based on free will.

To produce such a constitutional change, there would have had to be neither conqueror nor conquered; for this war was by nature not one of conquest but of unity. On the contrary, all conquests were purely fortuitous in character, and it was the victor's misfortune that he did not see this.

Thus Germany repeated the errors of Versailles. As once people had spoken of the League of Nations, so they now spoke of the New Europe, which was basically merely the imperial disguise of a militant national state, but not a league based on the equal rights and duties of all. Therefore Germany had to bear alone the burden of the struggle and seek support by employing force, which propaganda cloaked with increasing adroitness but with diminishing effect.

It was particularly depressing that relations between Germany and France deteriorated; here immediately after the armistice there was a period when it was recognized and acknowledged to what extent the two lands are made to supplement each other, and how much they were disposed at heart to enter a new order.

The meager resistance which the armies had offered compared with the fighters of Douamont bore witness that the conflict was no longer conceived as a fight to the death. France, considered as a national state, had exhausted itself in the tremendous sacrifices of the First World War. On the other hand, unlike England it drew no power to invigorate its thoughts and actions from realms of empire.

In Germany, on the contrary, the element of nationalism was not yet exhausted. Therein lies the reason why the struggle was renewed and now seemed to be assuming its final form; the reason being that Germany had to lose the war of conquest which she waged as a national state — and correspondingly one saw the forces of resistance grow in proportion as her efforts increased. Now it is important that along with the others she should win the war in so far as it is a war of unity.

Yet the speedy conclusion of the war in France spared much for mankind. Thus the destruction of Paris, that irreplaceable masterpiece, was avoided. May it after the deluge, like an ark laden deep with things of age and beauty, make landfall at a new haven for the delight of future generations!

It will be recognized too that the occupation, in spite of all the sufferings it brought, also left seeds of friendship. It is true that almost everything which was attempted between the states as such was a failure for lack of freedom, which is the source of concord. Nor were there lacking infringements of rights, distortions of justice, deeds of violence of all kinds. It is important for both that they should be atoned.

Yet the best of the peoples came to know each other, for such fateful times ever offer occasion for help. Respect, friendship, and love, too, spin a web of fine threads which will endure for more than many a treaty between the nations.

IX

In the meantime, terrible lessons showed man the way to an ordered life. If this does not find expression in a new league, in a new life lived in unity and in accordance with higher laws; if, instead, passions trouble the peace, then the drama through which we live will be repeated in a more violent form.

Man must never forget that the images which now terrify him are drawn from his heart. The world aflame, the burnt-out houses, the ruined towns, the trails of destruction are like leprosy whose germs had long multiplied within before it broke out on the surface. Such have long been the images in the hearts and minds of men. It is the innermost stuff of man's being which is reflected in the world around us, just as inner composure is revealed by external calms. Therefore spiritual salvation must come first, and only that peace can bring a blessing which has been preceded by the taming of the passions in these hearts and minds of men.

This must be borne in mind when it comes to punishing the guilty. It will be those who are firm of purpose but weak in judgment who will push themselves forward as judges. Therefore it is important that here reason and knowledge of the whole problem should hold sway, but not blind party vengeance which adds new injustice to old.

You must know that in such conflicts there is a large element of destiny; like whirlpools they draw men in and lead them to new goals. Yet man is always required to distinguish between justice and injustice and to resist crime, even at his own peril. Evil cannot be excused because it was enforced or because the times called for it. To such instances the words of St. Matthew apply:

"For it must needs be that offenses come, but woe to the man by whom the offense cometh."

Yet revenge, passion must on no account play the leading role. Avenging the victims is much less important than the restoration of justice and in particular of the sense of justice which over wide stretches of the earth has been dulled and suppressed. The determination to create justice must have order and healing as its aim. There must be no more parts of the earth where fear reigns and men live exposed without just sentence to assault on their persons and on their lives, on their possessions and their freedom In this respect, justice is like a light penetrating far into the surrounding dark.

For this reason it is undeniably important that justice should be meted out. The sense of justice does not die utterly in any people, and revives mightily when it is demonstrated that injustice cannot endure, and that crime finds condign punishment, whatever the tyranny under which it was committed. For this to become fully apparent, neither parties nor nations should sit in judgment on their opponents. The plaintiff cannot also be judge.

It is to be foreseen that the terrible gulfs which violence has opened will not close without outbursts of vengeance on the part of the oppressed. Yet justice cannot be achieved in that way; the evil deeds can be expiated only where hatred does not dictate the verdict. Only then can it be distinguished who is to be considered as soldier and who as hangman, who as warrior and who as murderer, and which of the opponents in the war of nations is worthy of respect as a foe or of the gallows as a shedder of innocent blood. But if partisans make the distinction, then they convert criminals into martyrs and national heroes.

That is not to say that justice must not be thorough. There is too much stupid, senseless tyranny and oppression of the defenseless, too many executioners and their assistants, too many torturers great and small, for the gulf to close before justice has been measured out in full.

But it is important that the crimes should stand revealed for all time; and that will be possible only by justice, never through revenge. Justice is by nature like a light which intensifies the shadows. The less justice draws its inspiration from the passions, the more clearly the crime stands out in its ugliness.

X

Expiation is one of the presuppositions of the new league; purification precedes unification.

The peace itself, however, must be entirely dedicated to the future. In it must be realized the aims inherent in the war as a whole. Through it the earth presses on to new forms in which all powers cooperate. Therefore in each party, even if hidden under the dross of violence, there lies hid a good claim to justice. The task is to bring it to the surface and realize it in a loftier form.

If we consider dispassionately the aims which are being fought for, we will find that almost all the problems which exercise the human race are playing their part. Three questions of prime importance can, however, be distinguished; to these the peace must be expected to find a solution. The first is the question of living space, for there are certain powers which are fighting for space — those which are also called the totalitarian states. The fact that they are on the move is a sign that the division of the earth, as developed historically, requires to be altered. Therefore no peace promises to be of long duration which does not allay this unrest in a just manner. Yet these demands, which are based on natural justice, must be satisfied on a higher plane — not by conquests but by alliances. The earth must provide bread for all.

The second great question is that of justice — in so far as certain other powers claim to be fighting for justice. Undoubtedly the curtailment of rights which the totalitarian states have imposed upon men is not their internal affair alone. On the contrary, each encroachment upon freedom is seen abroad as a glaring threat. If the claim to participate justly in the territory and produce of the earth is well founded, so is the claim that the rights, liberties and dignity of man must be respected in all countries without exception. No other peace can last except that made between free peoples.

The third question, finally, is how the new way of life is to be achieved — that is, what shape the life of the workingman shall take. In this respect the nations have come to resemble each other closely and are becoming daily more alike; for the same great rhythm inspires the total mobilization on which they have embarked. This is not merely a question of a r m a m e n t s but of f a r - r e a c h i n g transformations. That the products of this labor process are delivered to the fronts is only one aspect of it; the other, invisible but no less effective, is at work within the nations themselves. Thus no nation will be demobilized in the same form as that in which it entered the war. War is the great forger of nations as it is of hearts.

The object of the peace is to reconcile these three great aims — they form the elements of its construction. The elements must support each other — thus it will be seen that the solution of the territorial question is intimately connected with the reform of justice. Solution of the one entails solution of the other. To cure the sickness of the land-hungry peoples is to give them the chance of reforming the laws, and thus the element of danger is removed. The forces which are released from making armaments will produce for all.

Again, to settle the questions of justice and territory correctly, things must be given a new significance; this can be imparted only by the new man, the worker — the man who has already drawn up great projects, and who alone is endowed with the audacity and the vision to plan universal peace. He alone can already think in terms of continents; his concepts and symbols alone are comprehensible on a planetary scale. Therefore he will also be the ferment of unity.

The peace will have achieved its aims when the forces which are given over to total mobilization are freed for creation. Then the heroic age of the worker will have reached its fulfillment — the age which was also the age of revolutions. The angry torrent has hollowed out the bed in which peaceful waters will run. At the same time the figure of the worker, losing its titanic cast, will reveal new aspects of itself — then it will be seen what relation it bears to tradition, creation, happiness and religion.

XI

In all continents the territorial question will require to be settled. But the heart of the problem lies in Europe, from which as from the epicenter of a great earthquake the last three wars have radiated. Here, therefore, space to breathe is the first requirement.

Now each country will with justice endeavor not to become living space for others. Territorial adjustments can therefore not be achieved by force or by dictated terms, and no territory is gained by taking it from one to give to another.

The true solution lies in the treaty alone, in the league of peace, in the pooling of territory in accordance with new conceptions. Only this can obviate the cycle of hordes of armaments-workers followed by armies of unemployed, which every regime after the old model threatens to reproduce. The nations will bring whatever territory they possess as dowry. It will become evident that on this basis it is possible to live better, more richly, and — above all — more safely than before.

Europe must be created out of its separate members; then will come new life, freer breath, a more spacious era. Man is confronted by a Promethean task. Yet forerunners and precedents are not lacking. Among them is the creation of the unified state by Bismarck and Cavour. As the nations were born out of the dynasties and fragments of old empires, so today they in turn must coalesce to form an *imperium*. There is no lack of patterns or models: the world knows states where the most diverse nations, races and tongues are united. Among them are Switzerland, the United States, the Soviet Union and the British Empire. In these structures a mass of political experience has crystallized. To it we can have recourse.

To set up a European state means, therefore, to give geographical and political unity to territory which historical development was already shaping. The great difficulty lies in the long tradition, the peculiar ways of life which have grown up in its nations. This is what Goethe meant when he said in his day that America was more fortunate than our continent. The time has come, however, when the forms have become fluid and ready for recasting. It is a task which may now reasonably be set; the hopes of the nations rest upon it.

XII

Land hunger will be relieved by the unification of the nations: nor is there any more just solution. How they are to live together in their new home will be laid down in the constitution.

In this connection there is no point in going into details. Yet there are two supreme principles which must find expression in the constitution, irrespective of how they may be incorporated in it. These two principles are those of unity and of diversity. The new dominion must be a union of all its members, but must respect their individuality.

In this combination the two main trends which democracy has assumed in our time must be reconciled — that of the authoritarian and that of the liberal state. There is good reason for both; but life cannot be either entirely disciplined nor completely dominated by free will. It is rather a question of distinguishing the levels appropriate to each.

The forms of the authoritarian state apply where men and things can be organized technically. On the other hand, freedom must have control where more organic processes are the rule. It is thus that nature fashions shellfish, with a hard, gleaming embossed shell and a delicate interior in which the pearls are hidden. In this differentiation lies the welfare of states and the happiness of individuals.

There should be uniformity of organization in whatever concerns technical matters, industry, commerce, communications, trade, weights and measures, and defense. These departments are like the great roads and railways which run gleaming across an empire and are the same in all its provinces whatever the nature of the country or its people. Man is a child of his time, and as a civilized being can move along them without striking barriers and will everywhere find himself at home.

Liberty, on the other hand, dominates in diversity — wherever nations and men differ. That applies to their history, their speech and race, to their customs and habits, their art and their religion. Here there cannot be too many colors on the palette.

Thus the European constitution must skilfully distinguish the cultural plane from that of material civilization, forming them into picture and frame so as to unite their benefits for the human race. It must create territorial and political unity while preserving historical diversity. That implies at the same time distinguishing between the technical and the organic world. The state as supreme symbol of technical achievement takes the nations in its toils, yet they live in freedom under its protection. Then history will take a hand and give new contents to old forms. Europe can become a fatherland, yet many homelands will remain within its territories.

Within this framework the nations large and small will flourish more strongly than before. As the rivalry of the national states dies away, the Alsatian, for instance, will be able to live as German or as Frenchman without compulsion from one or the other. But above all he will be able to live as an Alsatian, as he wishes. This regained freedom will dawn even for racial minorities, for septs and towns. In the new home it will be possible to be Breton, Wend, Basque, Cretan or Sicilian — and that with greater freedom than in the old.

XIII

The peace must not be founded solely on human reason. It cannot endure if limited in its nature to a legal pact formed between men, if it does not also exist as a holy covenant.

Yet only thus is the deepest source of evil to be reached, that which springs from nihilism. What do treaties avail if there is to be no alteration here? We have seen empires adorned with lofty buildings and daring structures, which today are turned into heaps of rubble. Once again it is evident that no blessing rests upon Babylonian works.

It is no mere chance that nihilism was depicted philosophically by Nietzsche and in the novel by Dostoyevsky; for if it has been to school in all countries it was in Germany and Russia that it took up its abode. Therefore it was here that the changes were most far-reaching. And therefore it was between these two peoples that the war assumed its purest form.

That is all the more surprising since experience showed how much both nations are adapted to intercourse and what a blessing for both friendship brings. On them the peace of the world can rest as if on the shoulders of Atlas. Yet as technical thought found expression in human form the waves of fear that beat to and fro between them grew stronger. They surged between East and West like an echo which amplifies voices and renders them inhuman. The Russians began in earnest at a point where in Europe things were kept in the germ, in theory, or where antidotes discovered in the course of history had checked the monstrous growth. Then the fear radiating from the East gave to the nihilism which for generations had been maturing in Germany practical reality. It horrified not only the rest of the world but even those who knew their native land intimately.

In this case the only possible salvation was that which lies hidden in suffering. That is the reason why the new order could not be created by reasonable negotiations and by treaty-making, although the wounds of the First World War still bled. Those who dreamt of power and domination were led on by the path which goes down to destruction, the path which is described in Psalm 73.

Thus in spite of all tribunals and treaties we will plunge deeper into destruction if the transformation remains purely humanitarian and is not accompanied by a theological one. Yet there is hope of great changes. For instance, the Russian revolution stands on the brink of developing new phenomena, and there are many indications that having begun as a technical and political transformation it will find its final accomplishment in metaphysics. This destiny has not only been described in detail by the great writers of that country, but can also obviously be divined from the Russian himself, whom technical developments have affected as superficially as they have the surface of his earth. He has yet to reap the harvests. In the course of this transformation, security will radiate from him as once did fear.

Similarly the German still has strong reserves in the background. They will reveal themselves when the technocrats abdicate; Then it will be apparent what spirit, nobility, truth and goodness live in that people. Then, too, it will be seen what courage was required to remain German in these years — courage which had to exceed by far that shown at the front in its opposition to the powers of destruction, of whose secret terrors the world has as yet no conception. In East and West the fame of martyrs will shine out, whose names are still hidden in the hearts of the people.

The nations will recognize each other in their true form when the specters of hate have vanished which evil requires for its rule. Thus it will be obvious what share France must have in any unification. For long the spirit of that country has been striving towards greater unity in which its labors too will be crowned. For the French, the step of becoming a good European will be the least painful of all, will entail the least change, for in this respect they are the most advanced both spiritually and in their way of life. Their store of controlled energy corresponds to the Germans' excess of uncontrolled power, and both far exceed their own requirements. Admittedly here too it will be difficult to banish the shadow of the war. To accomplish the necessary tasks will require the best brains and corresponding courage.

As for as the return to practical affairs after weapons have given their decision is concerned the Briton possesses the most fortunate temperament, as Washington Irving so excellently showed in his sketch-book under the heading "John Bull." Therefore where cool commonsense and sound judgment are required, there is much to be hoped for from that country. For it is set upon long peaceful development and therefore only a unifying peace can be of advantage to it. Then, too, its traditional policy will alter or have a different stress in so far as from now on it is directed towards the unity of the European nations instead of on their differences; for world order is no longer maintained by the balance of powers, but of continents and empires.

At the moment when Europe raises itself to the status of a continent, the gravitational pull of America will become more perceptible. With the destruction of our towns, Goethe's saying has ceased to apply to this extent, that America now possesses the tradition of construction which we require. Napoleon prophesied that in our day the world would become republican or Cossack. If he had foreseen our situation in detail he would have said "American or Russian," as Tocqueville, too, long ago foretold. Although America, like Russia, will exert a powerful influence on Europe, neither of these two possibilities will be realized. Against them is the immense gravitational force of history, the treasure of old heritage, which has not only been formed by the spirit or art but still lives in men. Considered thus, the great empires of the past were something in the nature of potentialities which Europe realized from itself, vital motives from its spirit and blood. That will be particularly marked in the great changes that will take place — just as it was apparent in the influence of America on the declaration of human rights. And so too Europe stands in need of another Lafayette to advise on the great territorial and constitutional questions that accompany the union of its states.

XIV

If the struggle against nihilism is to succeed, it must be fought out in the heart of each one of us. Everyone shared in the guilt, and there is no one who did not stand in need of the healing powers which are to be found in the realms of suffering.

To this end, it is necessary that in the life of the individual as in the constitution technical knowledge should be kept in its place. The modes and methods of technical thinking must not encroach where human happiness, love and well-being should flourish. The intellectual, the titanic powers must be separated from the human and the divine and subordinated to them.

That is possible only if men strengthen themselves metaphysically in proportion to the growth of technical science. And here begin the wide, virgin fields of the new theology; it is the first among the sciences, for it is knowledge of the deepest causes and of the highest law which shaped the world.

Since the time of Copernicus, a wider vision of the universe has opened out, and with it have opened the portals to realms of evil, to purely mechanical insect-life and to murderous anarchy, such as was foreseen by Bosch and his school. That these portals will close is foreshadowed in those sciences which round off and define mental horizons. Those who today belong to the elite — be it as philosophers, artists, or scientists — are nearest to the mysteries, to the point where perception must give way to revelation.

At the same time, the danger has become so great that each one of us must be asked to take a decision, that is, to make a confession of faith. We have reached the point where, if not belief, at least piety, an effort to live justly in the highest sense of the word, can be demanded of mankind. Tolerance must have limits to this extent, that the leadership of men cannot be granted to the nihilists, to the pure technicians or to those who despise all moral obligations. Whoever places his trust in man and human wisdom alone cannot speak as judge, nor can he expound as teacher, heal as doctor or serve the state as official. These are modes of life that end with hangmen in the seats of the mighty.

The state therefore acts in its own interests if it not only advances the great doctrines of salvation, but places its trust in those of its citizens who confess to belief in an intelligence transcending man's. To the extent that this comes about we will see nihilism decline, the desert shrink — just as persecution on grounds of faith flourished when nihilism was strongest.

The state must ever look to faith if it is not quickly to fall in ruin or be destroyed by fire. Thus we have seen it exact homage to strange idols — to theories which were the stock in trade of country schoolmasters fifty years ago, to materialistic philosophies and to the scribblings of puffed, empty heads, to its machines and to its great engineering works: in short to spiritual fetishes of all kinds. And one saw propaganda untiringly busy patching up this motley raiment which the healthy mind unravelled like Penelope's weft. Dreams have more substance than this wind.

Mankind is willing and it will be well worth while to turn him from folly to the truth.

XV

The view is still widely held that to re-establish order it would suffice to return to the liberal state. But that would merely mean returning to our point of departure. In the polemics which the old Liberals sustain against the nihilists, they behave like fathers bewailing their misguided children without seeing that the real fault lies in inadequate education. Just as useless is the criticism of those who watched the terrible contest from the safety of the gallery.

The true conquest of nihilism and the attainment of peace will be possible only with the help of the churches. Just as the trustworthiness of a man in the new state will depend not on his internationality, but on his nationality, so his education must aim at adherence to a faith and not at indifference. He must know his native land on earth and in the infinite, in time and in eternity. This education for a full life must have its roots in loftier certainties than the state can establish with its schools and universities.

In addition the churches, too, stand in need of a revival, in the sense that implies return to fundamentals; for true recovery, new life must go back to the sources. Admittedly that is possible only under a temporal guise and so it is through new forms that theology has to work upon mankind.

Modern man is determined to believe; that he has demonstrated by the very strength with which he has clutched at absurdities, at fleeting phantasms of the mind. Yet he is a rational being who must be brought to salvation in a rational manner. If it is to be equal to the task, theology must no longer be a second class subject in the curriculum. Rather must theology as the prince of sciences attract not only the best hearts, but the best minds too, the purest intellects — those which find no satisfaction in the discipline of the individual sciences nor even in philosophy, but which are commensurate with the totality of things, with the universe.

Then it will no longer be a question of refuting the results of the various sciences, but of evaluating them, of transcending them after the manner of Pascal. Only then will the sciences bear fruit not in terms of the spirit but actually in terms of economics; then they will be insured against the strange loss which, in spite of increases in technical efficiency, has more and more robbed man of his gains. It is as if man were pouring water into a jug without seeing that it lies in fragments. Such a state of affairs can be set right only by intellects which are at home in the whole of creation; only there is overflowing plenty.

This explains why the state must give theology precedence above all research and study — for it is research of the utmost validity. The state, like all works fashioned by the hand of man, must take its measure against the mighty structure of creation.

XVI

Diversity of peoples, races and nations — besides these Europe can also possess a diversity of churches, no matter with what rites and symbols they worship. None must be prevented from adhering to the faith of his fathers or to that to which he has been converted. Even if it should be demanded of a man that he have a transcendental idea, he must be free to choose the manner in which he elevates himself to it.

In Europe, however, the state church can only be the Christian church. Its claim is supported by the fact that in it is to be found the strongest of the old ties which have survived the era of national separatism. Within it is preserved the greatest sum of faith that yet survives. Amidst the universal conflagration and in the maelstrom of nihilism it revealed itself as a power which still protected the weal of numberless persons, not only from its pulpits and altars, but in the cathedrals of the intellect, in its doctrine and in the aura which surrounds the faithful and does not forsake them even in the hour of death. New martyrs bore witness for it.

Mankind had to learn that in the midst of the catastrophe none of the subtle systems and none of his teachings and writings could give him counsel — or at least only for ill. They all lead to murder and the cult of power. On the other hand in the whirlwinds of destruction, the truth of the great images of Holy Scripture became ever clearer — of its commandments, promises and revelations. In the symbols of the divine origin of the world, of the creation, of mans fall, in the images of Cain and Abel, of the flood, of Sodom and Gomorrah and of the tower of Babel, in the psalms and in the prophets, and in the truth of the New Testament which transcends the base laws of the realm of terror — in all these is manifested to us the eternal framework which is the foundation of human history and human geography. Hence it is on this book that all oaths of alliance must be sworn as the men of Pitcairn island swore, survivors of shipwreck on a Pacific isle. They hunted each other there like wolves, until their higher nature finally brought them to peace.

On that island it was recognized that a return to fundamentals was a moral necessity and on them they founded their social order. That is indicated in our case also. The people must be brought back to Christian morals, without which they are rendered as defenseless prey to destruction. There lies mankind's path — imitation of man's great prototype; but the path will be useless unless at the same time, high above mere moral law, a way is found to the divine image. That is a path which only the elite may tread.

XVII

For these reasons the peace treaty cannot merely take the shape of a constitution in accordance with national and international law — a constitution in which questions of justice, territory and precedence are settled; it must also bear fruit in a religious covenant.

The unity of the West, realized for the first time since the empire of Charlemagne, must not be confined to the assimilation of countries, peoples and cults, but must come to life again in the church. The reformation has need of the church as the church has of reformation. Streams which have flowed in separate channels must be again united.

That is the high goal; merely to recognize it and to have it in view is no small thing. This the churches had already done, for they made common cause in the fight against nihilism, and this fellowship must be crowned for all to see when the complex organism on which they live unites its members in a single body.

XVIII

It is the mark of a just peace that it gives full expression to the spirit of the times. That spirit it must make manifest in politics, in things of the spirit, in the doctrine and rites of religion — and that irrespective of whether this or that group of powers has emerged victorious, irrespective of whether the fight is fought out to the end or whether subtle diplomacy contrives to spare the peoples part of the ordeal.

Yet it is better to fight longer and suffer longer than to return to the old world. Let the towns be laid low if they know neither justice nor freedom, let the cathedrals crash in ruin if there is no reverence in them. Peace is desirable only if it embraces whatever works of man still have some worth and dignity.

But. should the final word be with mere commonsense acting in accordance with technical principles, then the conclusion of the war will be only apparent. It will turn to civil war, to pure butchery. Tyranny and with it fear will grow and darkness spread further abroad; then after an even shorter interval than before new fronts and new conflicts will ripen.

It should be borne in mind that the technique for developing the powers imprisoned in the elements is still progressing. And thereby the possibilities of destruction will also increase. Today they attempt to strike at the masses of the population, a fact which has become particularly evident by the attacks on the cities. But already there are signs of the desire to go beyond that, to achieve total annihilation — that is, to destroy life altogether. So today dreams of exterminating whole countries and whole groups of peoples already form part of the nihilist's ideology.

That is the prospect which nihilism has to offer — the great triumph of death after which it yearns. It is a spirit which you may recognize by its diabolical lusts — which the majority applaud — lusts after hatred, disunity and destruction.

XIX

The question remains: What can the individual contribute to the peace? It is all the more urgent since today the individual tends to underestimate the importance of the role assigned to him.

The rage of the elements makes him despair of his power; he lets his hands drop in face of the conflagration. By renouncing his free will he renders himself helpless and thereby subject to fear and the powerful forces of evil whose might lies in the interplay of hate and terror. They think to make man their instrument and are waiting only for the kind of wild exultation with which he shall assume full responsibility. Thus he adopts a position in which he loses the power to differentiate between good and evil and becomes only a plaything of his passions.

The answer to this is that the responsibility of the individual is tremendous, and that no one can relieve him of it. The world must answer before his court and he is judge of right and wrong.

Therefore today more than ever before he can do good. The world is full of violence, of men persecuted, imprisoned and suffering. How easily and with what scanty means can one bring comfort, assuage the suffering and give protection! Even the least of us has the opportunity, and the service rendered grows in proportion to the limited powers at one's disposal. True power is to be recognized by the protection it affords.

Above all the individual must recognize that peace cannot grow out of lassitude. Fear, too, contributes to war and its prolongation. Only thus can one explain the outbreak of the Second World War so soon after the first. To have peace it is not enough not to wish for war. True peace postulates courage of a higher order than that which war demands; it is a product of spiritual travail, of spiritual strength. It is attained when we learn to extinguish the red fires within us and to free our own hearts from hate and its disruptive power.

Thus each one of us is like a light which as it grows overcomes the surrounding gloom. A little light is greater, has more power than thick darkness.

That is true also of those who are destined to fall. They pass in goodly fellowship through lofty portals into eternity. The real struggle in which we are involved is more and more clearly that between the powers of destruction and the powers of life. In that fight the fighters for justice stand shoulder to shoulder like the chivalry of old.

The more fully this finds expression the more enduring will be the peace.

Milton Keynes UK
Ingram Content Group UK Ltd.
UKHW021030231024
2330UKWH00043B/285